# A Day at Rainbow Lake

**Written by** Linda Cave

STECK-VAUGHN
COMPANY

*A Division of Harcourt Brace & Company*

It is a day in May at Rainbow Lake.
The lake is home to many animals.

Ducks live at Rainbow Lake. Do you see the male duck? He is called a drake.

Fish live at Rainbow Lake, too. They swim to the top of the lake. They take a look for bugs.

This crane lives at Rainbow Lake. It wades into the water. It looks for crayfish and insects to eat.

Beavers live at Rainbow Lake. They use trees to make a home. Their home is called a lodge.

The beavers swim in the lake. When danger is near, they make a loud sound. They slap their tails down on the water.

Rainbow Lake is a good place for foxes. Foxes do not swim in the lake. They come to take a drink of water.

Rainbow Lake is a good place for deer, too. They come to the lake to take a drink. They come early and late in the day.

This snake lives at Rainbow Lake. It likes to stay warm. It looks for a place in the sun. It may stay on a warm rock all day long.

Here is a snail at Rainbow Lake. It leaves a little trail behind. All snails like to stay in the shade.

Rainbow Lake has lots of frogs. The frogs swim in the lake. They hop from place to place.

The frogs sit in one place, too. They wait for bugs to pass by. They make a meal out of the bugs.

Rainbow Lake has raccoons, too. Raccoons have brown and gray fur on their body. The black fur on their face looks like a mask.

Raccoons sleep all day. They stay in their den and rest. They come out late at night. Baby raccoons love to play.

This girl lives at Rainbow Lake. Her name is Kayla. She thinks Rainbow Lake is the best place to stay. Would you like to spend a day at Rainbow Lake?